GROW UP GREAT!

ALL YOU NEED TO KNOW ABOUT
PUBERTY FOR GIRLS

BY OLIVIA KEY AND LAURA WOOD

W
FRANKLIN WATTS
LONDON • SYDNEY

CONTENTS

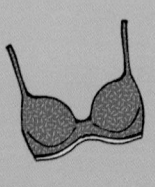

READY, STEADY ... PUBERTY!

Hands up if you would like to find out about puberty! You would? Excellent. Because this book contains all the facts that you'll need. So read on to find out how to grow up great. **Go!**

WHAT EVEN IS PUBERTY?

Puberty is the name for the stage in your life when you change from a girl into a woman. It happens to all girls, so you're not on your own. (Psst. It happens to boys, too.) Here's a sneak preview of what to expect:

- You'll grow bigger and taller.
- Your breasts will develop.
- Your hips will grow wider.
- You'll grow hair in new places.
- Your emotions will change.
- You'll probably get spots.
- Your periods* will start.

* If you're not sure what periods are, don't worry. There'll be lots of information about them later.

Don't worry! These changes don't just happen overnight. You won't wake up one morning to discover that you've got breasts the size of pumpkins and your underarm hair is so long that you can plait it.

TAKING ITS TIME ...

Instead, many of the changes you experience will be v-e-r-y gradual, which means you'll have lots of time to deal with each exciting new development. And for any events that might happen suddenly (periods, we're looking at YOU), you can be super prepared.

That's where this book can help. It will describe all the incredible things that are about to happen to you and what they mean, for you. Then you'll know exactly what to do when things start to happen!

WHAT'S THE POINT OF PUBERTY?

If puberty didn't happen, everyone would stay children for ever. No one would become an adult and no more children would be born.

Basically, the human race would come to a catastrophic full stop. Eeeeek!

TIME FOR A (BODY) CHANGE

Puberty is the process your body goes through to change you into someone who is able to have a baby. Before puberty, you can't have a baby. Afterwards, you can. But don't worry, just because you can have a baby doesn't mean you have to right now. There's plenty of time in the future. And if you don't feel like it, you never need to have a baby. Puberty just makes it possible to have a baby. One day. Maybe.

For boys, puberty doesn't mean that they can magically have a baby. But it does mean that their bodies change so that they can become fathers. Again, one day. Again, maybe.

NOT RIGHT NOW, THANKS!

FACT OR FICTION?

It's just humans who go through puberty.

FICTION!

Animals go through puberty too! In fact, all species go through puberty, as they become adults who are able to reproduce, or have young. And like humans, puberty affects animals in different ways. During puberty, chimpanzees go through a growth spurt. Afterwards, as they get used to their suddenly bigger bodies, they are clumsy and awkward.

WHEN DOES PUBERTY START?

Ah. Unfortunately, there's not an exact answer to that question.

SAVE THE DATE!

Obviously, it would be very useful if puberty started on a particular day, so you knew when to expect it. But although no one knows exactly when puberty will start, there is a helpful age range.

For girls, puberty usually starts between the ages of 8 and 13. For boys, it's a little later. Puberty usually kicks off between the ages of 9 and 14.

For a few people, puberty can start earlier or later than those ages, too. So that's literally YEARS when puberty might – and might not – begin. Which means that the chances of predicting the moment when puberty will start for YOU are fairly low. (Sorry about that.)

The good thing is that puberty doesn't jump out and surprise you with a big TA-DAAAAAA. It's far less showy. In fact, puberty can begin so slowly that you might not even realise that anything is actually happening at first. Until, one day, it is.

WHAT MAKES PUBERTY HAPPEN?

Phew! There IS an exact answer to this question. Puberty begins because of GnRH.

And while you might suspect this is the sound a grumpy grandad makes when you've woken him from a snooze, it actually stands for something far more exciting. GnRH is short for Gonadotropin-Releasing Hormone. (See, properly thrilling!)

THE ACTUAL SCIENCE

So what are hormones? Quite simply, these are chemicals that carry messages around the body, like tiny couriers. GnRH is the hormone that tells your reproductive system – the parts of your body that work together to make babies – what to do and when to do it.

Children have low levels of GnRH. When GnRH levels increase … BOOM. Puberty begins! In girls, GnRH kickstarts the production of oestrogen. This hormone has a starring role in puberty – and beyond.

How do you think oestrogen helps your body?
Make wild guesses in this mini quiz!

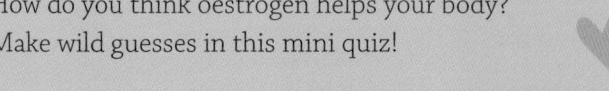

1.   It makes periods happen.

2.   It strengthens bones.

3.   It makes muscles strong.

4.   It keeps the heart healthy.

5.   It makes skin glow.

Answer: Oestrogen is responsible for ALL of these
amazing things. It really is that important.

THE FIRST SIGNS

For girls, the very first clue that puberty
has started is usually that their breasts
begin to develop.

Try not to panic though. They don't grow instantly!
Instead, the first stage is that breast buds appear.
A breast bud is a bump found beneath each nipple.
(For lots more on breasts, check out pages 20–27.)

DID YOU KNOW...?

- Each breast bud is about as big as a medium-sized coin.
- They might feel hard, itchy, sore or swollen.
- Sometimes, one grows faster than the other.
- Eventually, each breast bud will grow into a breast.

IT'S NOT JUST YOU

It's NO fun being the very last person in your friend group to show any signs of puberty. If this is you, you might feel as if you're missing out. You might even be a bit worried. And it's quite possible that you're fed up of annoying adults telling you not to worry. They'll probably say puberty will happen sooner or later. And they are right – it will. But if you're feeling fed up because it seems that the whole world is experiencing puberty before you, spare a thought for the people who start puberty first. They might feel fed up, too!

FROM GIRLS TO WOMEN

You've probably noticed that women are quite different to girls. And it's not just because they don't go to school, wear too much navy blue and go on about the importance of going to bed early while staying up way too late themselves. Their bodies look different, too.

GOING UP

During puberty, girls grow taller, quite quickly. This growth spurt usually happens at an earlier age than it does for boys, so if you've ever longed to be the tallest in the class, now's the time to enjoy the moment! (If you're not the tallest, sneak a pair of platform trainers into school and you soon will be.) You'll grow fastest from the time breast buds appear until a few months before your periods start. Then, just as you might begin to think that the only job you'll ever be qualified for is Very Tall Basketball Player, things slow down.

GOING OUT ... AND IN

Your hips will get wider, too. There's a very good reason
for this. It happens because the pelvis – a ring of bones
that includes your hip bones – begins to grow bigger
so that your body is able to carry a baby and give birth.
At the same time, your waist might get narrower.

GETTING CURVIER

While you're going through puberty, you might notice
that you're a little curvier in places like your bottom,
stomach, thighs, upper arms and even your upper back.
Don't worry! This is all absolutely normal. Your body
simply needs a little extra fat in order to grow.

WHAT WILL I LOOK LIKE AFTER PUBERTY?

According to pages 14 and 15 of this incredibly wise book, after puberty, you'll be taller, with wider hips and a curvier body. And so will every other girl.

So, you might be wondering, if the same things happen to all girls ... then why do all women look SO different?

GENE GENIE!

Even though hormones mastermind puberty, they don't get to decide the shape of your nose or the size of your breasts or a million other things. That's all thanks to genes.

Genes are the pieces of information you carry inside the cells in your body that determine what you'll be like. You don't get a choice, by the way. (Sorry about that.) Genes are inherited from your birth parents.

FACT OR FICTION?

You can inherit curly hair.

FACT!

There are lots of things that you can't inherit, such as ball-catching skills, a love of broccoli and great table manners. But there are many, many characteristics than you can largely blame on your birth parents and curly hair is one. Here are a few more ...

- Eye colour
- Skin tone
- Freckles
- Blood group
- Being tall
- Right- or left-handedness.

EMBARRASSING ADULTS

You know how it goes. If you haven't seen a relative for a while, they are guaranteed to say THE most toe-curling things if you've changed even a little bit.

Here are a few. Score ten points for each one that a grown-up has said to you.

"Where does the time go?"
(It's as if grown-ups don't own watches, clocks or calendars.)

"Haven't you grown!"
(Surely it would be weirder if you hadn't?)

"I remember when you were this big!"
(Just imagine if you replied that you remember when they were younger?!)

Grown-ups don't usually mean to be embarrassing. If they haven't seen you for a while, they might not be sure what to say. They most likely don't know what you're interested in and might not have a clue about it anyway. (Give them a chance. They were probably born in the last century, after all.) And so instead they say the first thing that pops into their head, which is often to comment on how much you've changed since the last time you saw them. And if you're feeling even the tiniest bit self-conscious, this can make you feel even more awkward!

SO WHAT DO YOU DO?

It's simple. Help the ancient relative out by starting the conversation! Then they won't need to say embarrassing things to fill the silence.

1. Tell them about school. (Anything. Seriously, they're not fussy.)
2. Describe your latest hobby. (In detail.)
3. Ask them what they've been up to … then let THEM do the talking.

TALKING BREASTS

Nothing shouts puberty louder than breasts. They're one of the earliest things to develop. And because they're right under your nose, it's impossible to ignore them. Here's a handy breast questionnaire – a breastionnaire, if you like – to reveal the truth about them.

YES, I'VE STARTED PUBERTY. HOW DID YOU GUESS?

WHAT ARE BREASTS FOR?

Breasts are designed to feed babies. After a woman gives birth, this is where milk is made and stored. When a baby sucks a nipple, milk is released. Breasts perform exactly the same job as a baby's bottle of milk, but without the need to sterilise stuff and mix baby milk powder and water.

WHAT'S INSIDE?

Inside each breast, there's a circle of lobes that, if you could see through skin, would look like the petals of a flower. Within the lobes, glands called lobules produce milk, which is carried to the nipple in tiny tubes called ducts. Fibrous tissue and ligaments hold everything together, while fatty tissue fills the gaps in between.

ARE ALL BREASTS THE SAME SHAPE?

No. In fact, one set of breasts can look very different from another. They can be round, cone-shaped or teardrop-shaped, wide apart or squished close together. Nipples can point forwards, downwards, upwards or even in different directions. As for nipples, they can be any size and any colour (except maybe green). Everyone's different.

BONUS FACT

Did you know that the biological name for breast is "mammary gland"?

You do now!

BRING ON THE BRAS!

If your breasts have begun to grow, you might suddenly start to wonder if you need to wear a bra ... or not. When is the right time?

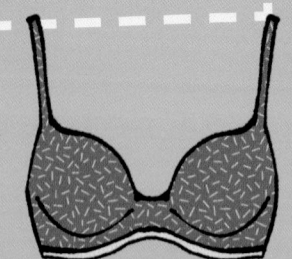

The answer is – whenever you like! A buzzer doesn't go off in the underwear section of your favourite shop to signal it's time for you to go shopping. And you don't need to wait until each breast is the size of, say, a satsuma or a digestive biscuit. If you feel as if you need to wear a bra or even if you just want to wear one, then it's the right time. Go for it!

YOUR VERY FIRST BRA

At first, it can be quite strange wearing a bra. So it's best to pick one that's as comfortable as possible. Luckily, there are some great choices out there!

Crop top, training bra or bralette

If your breast buds are tender or uncomfortable, then these lightweight bras will cushion them from accidental elbows and help you to feel more comfortable.

First bra

First bras are usually plain, simple, soft and comfortable. They might have padded cups to support you too.

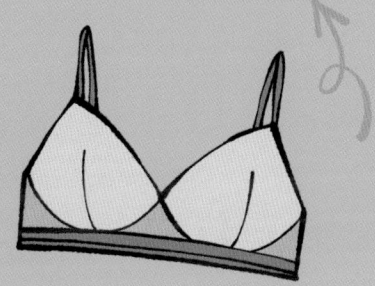

Sports bra

This type of bra will stop your breasts bouncing about in PE. And they aren't just useful during puberty. When you're older, it's still a good idea to wear these super-supportive bras when you're active.

FACT OR FICTION?

If the central band of your bra curves in the shape of a rainbow on your back, the bra doesn't fit properly.

FACT!

This shows that the bra is too big. The weight of your breasts might be pulling the bra down at the front, which means it rides up at the back.

BUYING YOUR FIRST BRA

(WITHOUT TURNING REDDER THAN A RED—HOT CHILLI PEPPER)

Choosing your first bra can be exciting, but it's totally normal to feel a little nervous too. So here are some handy hints for finding the right one as easily as possible.

1.   Take a trusted adult with you. This might be your mum, an auntie, a carer or a big sister. Whoever it is, this won't be the first time they've shopped for a first bra, so they'll know what to do.

2.   Remember that assistants in bra shops are not there to embarrass you. They're there to help you find the right bra. So do let them help you.

3. At first, it might look as if there are a billion bras to choose from, but there are probably only a few that are right for you. (The assistants know which ones these are.)

4. It's a great idea to be measured in a shop to find what size bra you need, but if the idea of this makes you curl into a tiny ball and shout, 'NOOOOO!', do it yourself before you go shopping. Use a soft fabric tape measure to measure the distance all the way round your chest and over your nipples. Now measure again underneath your breasts. Tell the assistant the numbers and – yay! – they'll magically be able to work out what size you are.

5. In the changing rooms of the shop, try on different bras in the right size. You might need to try quite a few until you find one that's just right, but keep going. You'll get there! Don't stop until you find one that's comfortable.

FITTING ROOM →

BRA-ILLIANT FACTS AND TOP ADVICE

Although they may feel a little weird at first, bras are designed to support you and to help you feel comfortable.

(They're also a great idea if you've got bigger breasts and want to take part in a 100-metre sprint.)

DID YOU KNOW ...?

• With bra sizes, the number – for example 28, 30, 32 or 34 – refers to the measurement round your body (under your breasts). Meanwhile, the letter – AA, A, B, C, D etc – refers to the size of your breasts. You might wear a bra that's 28AA, for example. Or your bra might be size 36D.

• Your breasts probably won't stay the same size throughout your life. They grow and shrink, depending on your weight and age. If you ever have a baby, they can grow much bigger. So, whenever you shop for a new bra, it's always worth checking your size, in case it's changed.

• 'Bra is short for 'brassiere', which is more difficult to spell.

IT'S NOT JUST YOU

What if every single girl you know is wearing a bra and your breasts haven't even started to grow yet ...?

Try not worry, they will appear sooner or later. And until they do, you can enjoy wearing halterneck or strapless tops without worrying about which bra to wear underneath. Besides, even if you really don't need a bra, crop tops are a great alternative to a vest.

Wear one anyway if you want to!

PUTTING SPOTS IN THE SPOTLIGHT

So, spots. Who gets them? When do they get them? Why and where do they get them? Let's find out more.

WHO?

If you're a human, then let's face it – you're probably going to be spotty from time to time. You might even be spotty already. And if you don't have spots, you're pretty much guaranteed to get them one day. If you're lucky enough to have totally clear skin, hurray!

WHEN?

Most people suffer from acne – the super-common skin condition that causes spots – at some point between the ages of 11 and 30. Girls often suffer from acne between 14 and 17. It can also happen around the time of your period (more on this later).

WHY?

Acne usually happens when hormones released during puberty make glands near your hair follicles produce much more oil. This oil affects the skin's balance and blocks pores, too. The result is: spots.

WHERE?

- The face is the number-one spot (sorry) to get acne. If you suffer with spots, you're probably going to get them here.
- The back takes the number-two spot (sorry, again).
- The chest is the third most popular spot (REALLY sorry …) for, erm, spots.

HOW?

How do you fix acne? With time, your spots might just go away on their own. But if they don't and the spots are bothering you, a pharmacist can recommend gels or creams that might work. If these don't work or you're very spotty and it's getting you down, a GP can help by prescribing something stronger.

QUIZ: SPOTS

Do you know your spot facts from fiction? Find out with this handy quiz!

1.   If you go near someone with spots, you'll catch them too.

2.   If you have spots it's because you're not washing your face properly.

3.   If you squeeze spots, they'll go away faster.

4.   Rubbing toothpaste on spots makes them magically disappear.

5.   Face washes cure spots.

ANSWER: They're all absolute NONSENSE. Don't believe ANY of them.

1.   Acne isn't infectious. If you go near someone with spots, you're not going to catch them too. (And imagine if you were the one with spots. Wouldn't it be awful if your friends avoided you ...?)

2.   Acne is caused by changes in your body and has nothing to do with how dirty – or clean – your face is. In fact, washing too often or scrubbing spots too roughly could irritate them and make them worse.

3.   Adults are particularly fond of saying this. Some of them might even offer to squeeze your spots for you. (Ewwww.) Don't listen to them! Squeezing spots can push bacteria deeper into your skin, causing scabs that might later scar.

4.   Toothpaste is for cleaning teeth. It's not for making spots disappear and might actually make them worse. Save it for your toothbrush.

5.   There's nothing wrong with washing your face, but as acne is a skin condition, soap isn't going to cure it.

HAIR EVERYWHERE!

When puberty starts, extra hair starts to show up in surprising new places. Hair will grow between your legs. It will also appear in your armpits.

But why? What's the point? And what's it FOR?!

UNDERARM HAIR

Hair grows under your arms because of hormones that are kickstarted by puberty. It might seem pointless, but armpit hair actually comes in pretty handy when you're running. If you're pumping your arms and powering along like an action hero, the skin under your arm can rub against skin on your body and make it sore. Because armpit hair is in between your arm and your body, it stops the skin rubbing together, reducing friction.

FACT OR FICTION?

You have to remove underarm hair.

FICTION!

There's absolutely no harm in leaving underarm hair exactly where it is. However, if the hair makes you self-conscious or you just don't like it, there are lots of ways of removing it.

Shaving with a razor is one of the easiest ways to do it, but ask an older sibling, parent or carer for advice first. Nicking yourself with a razor is not fun, but there are lots of razors, including electric razors, designed to make it easy to shave without cutting yourself.

Hair-removal cream is another simple way of removing the hair under your arms quickly and easily. All you do is wipe on the cream, wait a few minutes and then wipe it off again, along with the hair. Or, if you're really hardcore, you can wax.

SMELLY STUFF

Around the time your armpit hair starts to grow, you'll start to sweat more, too. Sweating is very important, as it keeps your body at the right temperature.

KEEP IT CLEAN

How this happens is really quite amazing. First, you sweat – especially from under your arms and from your forehead, your face, palms and feet – and then your body uses heat energy to turn the drippy, watery sweat into vapour, leaving you cooler afterwards. Clever, eh? What's not so clever is that although sweat itself isn't smelly, when it meets bacteria on your skin, then VOILA! The result is BO.

BO stands for body odour, which can be quite smelly indeed. Perhaps you've smelt someone else's BO and already know what it's like. Annoyingly, you can often miss your own BO, simply because your nose gets used to familiar smells. But, to avoid someone else pointing it out – literally THE most embarrassing thing ever – then the best way to curb BO is to hop in the bath or shower.

FACT OR FICTION?

Perfume banishes BO.

FICTION!

Throughout history, perfume has been used to make people smell nice. But, sadly, perfume doesn't get rid of BO.

You can wear nice smells, obviously. But it's more important to wash every day, using shower gel or soap. After you're nice and clean, wearing deodorant under your arms can help, too. It doesn't stop you sweating, but it does get rid of the bacteria that causes BO when you do sweat. Antiperspirants work by blocking sweat pores, which reduces sweatiness (and whiffiness).

HAIR DOWN THERE

When it starts to grow, the hair between your legs will be quite fine, but after a year or so it'll be thick, curly and darker than the hair on your head.

This hair is called pubic hair – because it covers a soft area that medical people call the mons pubis, which protects the pubic bone beneath.

WELL, HELLO DOWN THERE!

FACT OR FICTION?

If you don't trim your pubic hair, it will grow down to your knees.

FICTION!

Unlike the hair on your head, which can grow long enough for you to sit on, pubic hair only grows to a length of between 1cm and 4cm long.

You might hear a lot of discussion about what different people do with their pubic hair. If you're worried about stray pubic hairs poking out of the side of your pants or swimming costume, then there are ways of removing hair here and there. Some friends might shave the edges a little, some might use hair removal cream and others might wax, but the important thing to remember is that you don't actually have to do anything at all, unless you want to. It's totally up to you!

It's not just pubic hair that's down there, of course. Turn over for a closer look!

TAKE A CLOSER LOOK

Without a periscope, it's not exactly easy to see what's going on between your legs.

You'll already know that there's a hole where your wee comes out. The proper name for this is the urethra. And round the back is the hole where poo appears. This is the anus. But there's actually a third hole, too. This is ... drumroll ... the vagina! And it plays a starring role in puberty and beyond.

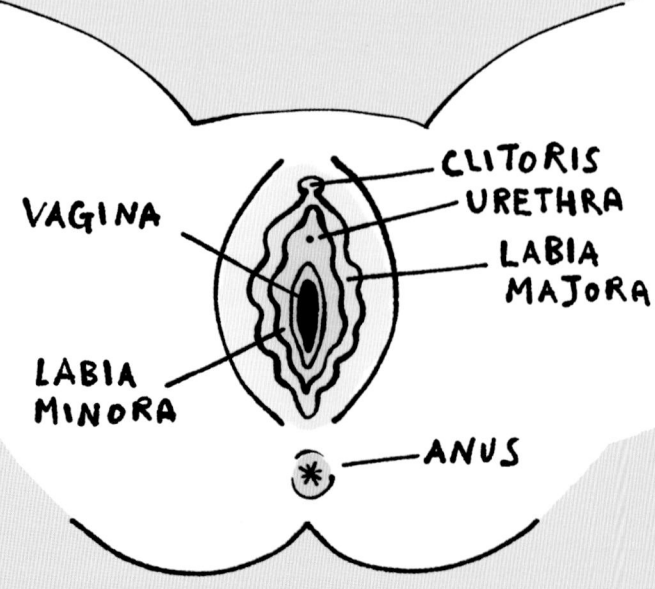

VAGINA

CLITORIS
URETHRA
LABIA
MAJORA

LABIA
MINORA

ANUS

AROUND THE VAGINA

And that's not all that's down there. Either side of the vagina, there are soft folds of skin called the labia (meaning lips). Their job is to keep the vagina safe from harm. There are two sets of labia to make sure everything is doubly protected. The labia majora are on the outside – these are the parts that can easily be seen. The labia minora are tucked inside the outer folds. Meanwhile, the clitoris is a small button-like part that sits inside the labia, in front of the urethra. Finally, the entire area is called the vulva.

IT'S NOT JUST YOU

If you'd like a closer look – and why not? It's your body, after all – you don't need a periscope, of course. A small mirror will do. But don't worry if everything doesn't look exactly like the diagram. Everyone is different!

The entire vulva is very sensitive, but the clitoris is the most sensitive part of all – it's not designed to do anything else except make you feel nice. Touching this area is something that you can do when you're on your own and is so normal that there's even a word for it – masturbation! Remember that no one else should ever touch you without your consent, though, even if it's someone you know well. If this happens, tell a parent or another trusted adult as soon as you can.

THE INSIDE STORY

Puberty is all about growing up – and obviously growing up great! You will see lots of the changes that happen on the outside, such as your breasts growing and hips widening, but at the same time, things are changing inside your body too ...

THE VIV (VERY IMPORTANT VAGINA)

Without a vagina, it would be pretty tricky to have a baby. Think of it like the swing doors at the front of a shop – it's both an entrance and an exit.

That's because the vagina is the way a man's sperm goes inside and it's also the way a baby usually comes out. Basically, the vagina links the uterus with the outside world. During puberty, the vagina, labia and clitoris all get bigger.

THE UTERUS

The uterus – also known as the womb – is where babies actually grow. It sits above the vagina. While you're going through puberty, the uterus gets bigger too, changing from a tube shape into a pear shape.

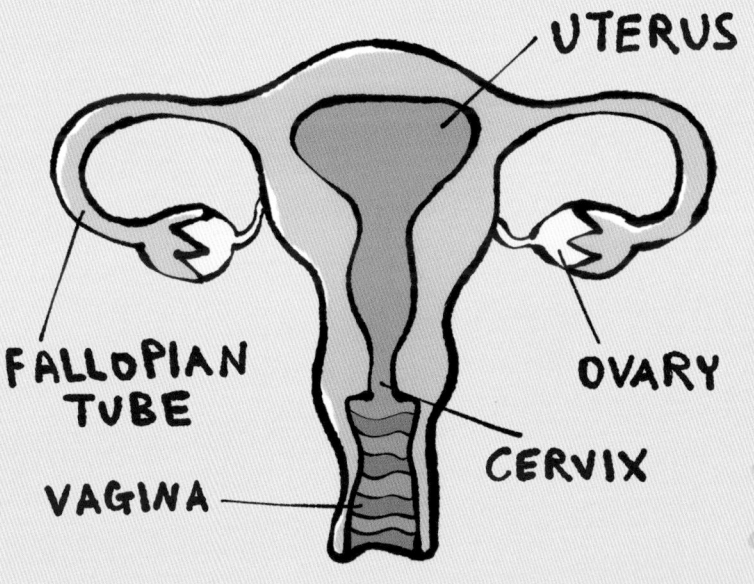

UTERUS

FALLOPIAN TUBE

OVARY

VAGINA

CERVIX

THE OVARIES

The ovaries are where eggs are stored. There aren't just a couple of dozen – you're born with between one and two million eggs! The fallopian tubes link the two ovaries to the uterus, where, if an egg is fertilised by a sperm one day, a baby will grow. During puberty, your ovaries will start to release one egg a month.

KNOW YOUR PERIODS

You've probably heard of periods. Maybe you've even whizzed straight to this page to find out more about them. If so, hello there!

On the other hand, perhaps you're already a period specialist and if there were a World Period Convention, you would be the keynote speaker. But no matter how much you know (or don't know), the topic of periods is probably a pretty hot one among you and your friends.

SO WHAT IS A PERIOD?

Quite simply, a period is when blood leaks from the vagina for a few days, roughly once a month. The fancy name for a period is menstruation, because it's part of the menstrual cycle. This has absolutely nothing to do with bikes and instead describes the monthly process that a uterus goes through.

During the menstrual cycle, an egg is released into the uterus by one of the ovaries. Meanwhile, the lining of the uterus thickens to make it a good place for a baby to grow. However, if the egg is not fertilised by a sperm, the thick lining of the uterus is not needed to provide a cosy home for a developing baby, so it begins to shed. That's a period!

FACT OR FICTION?

The length of time between the first day of a period and the first day of the next can be as short as 21 days and as long as 35 (and sometimes, it can be even shorter or longer!).

FACT!

Although the average number of days between the beginning of periods is about 28 days, you might have periods that are closer together or further apart.

WHAT TO EXPECT DURING A PERIOD

If you haven't started your periods yet, it can be a little scary listening to others' dramatic stories of blood, cramps, sanitary towels and tampons. And what even is a Moon Cup? (Clue - see page 49.)

So what are periods really like?

BEFORE YOUR PERIOD

There are often signs that a period is on the way. A few spots of blood might appear in your pants. You might feel a low-down ache that comes and goes. You might have sore breasts or feel bloated or sluggish or a bit sad. Some people feel one or two of these things, others all of them or none of them. And it might vary from month or month. Everyone's different and there are no set rules.

GO WITH THE FLOW

A period itself is probably much more bearable than you imagine. There are usually days when there is only a little blood, which may be brown or pink. On heavier days, the blood will be red. A period usually lasts about five days, but it can be as short as two days or as long as seven.

FACT OR FICTION?

Every period, you'll lose around 20ml of blood.

FACT!

It might look as if you're bleeding quite a lot – especially during the first two days of your period. But in reality it's usually between 20ml (not even enough to fill an egg cup) and 90ml (one and a half of those tiny espresso cups).

If you seem to be bleeding lots more than this though, for example if you need to change your pad, pants or tampon every hour or so, it's a good idea to talk to a doctor.

PERIOD PANTS AND PADS

When your first period actually arrives, the most important thing is to be prepared.

There are lots of products out there to help you. They're all different, so even if you don't like the sound of one product, there's bound to be another that will suit you. Let's take a look …

SANITARY TOWELS

Sanitary towels, or pads, are super easy to use. They are pads of soft material, designed to stick to the inside of your pants, where they soak up blood as soon as it appears. All you need to do is change them every few hours. Pads come in all sorts of shapes, so you can choose the type that feels most comfortable. They're made in different absorbencies, too. This means that you can use a thicker pad for days when there's more blood or during the night. At the very end of your period, you might want to use a panty liner instead. These are super-thin pads for very light flow.

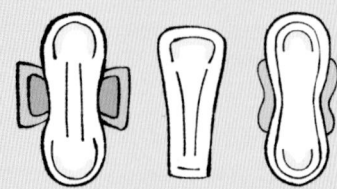

PERIOD UNDERWEAR

Period pants look like normal pants, but the gusset (inside layer) is made from fabric designed to hold on to moisture. So, during a period, blood doesn't leak into your clothes! After use, you can rinse period pants under running water, before washing them as usual. You can even get swimming period pants!

For even more choices, turn over!

TAMPONS AND MENSTRUAL CUPS

These period products sit inside your vagina and soak up or collect blood there. They can be more fiddly until you get used to them, so many girls use them when they're a bit older.

TAMPONS

The idea of tampons might seem a bit weird at first. They're tube-shaped and made of squashed cotton, but instead of being stuck to your pants like sanitary towels, tampons are pushed into the vagina and up. Here, they sit and absorb blood before it can leak out of your body. They can be a bit tricky to insert to begin with, but once you work out exactly where the tampon goes, they are very easy to use. Every packet has instructions to show you exactly what to do.

MENSTRUAL CUPS

Made from soft silicone, menstrual cups are designed to fit inside your vagina. They don't absorb blood – they collect it. A menstrual cup holds three times as much blood as a normal tampon and once it's been emptied and washed, you can pop it in again! Menstrual cups are made in different sizes, so you can choose one that fits. Like tampons, they can be a bit tricky to insert at first, so it's a good plan to get used to having periods before you try.

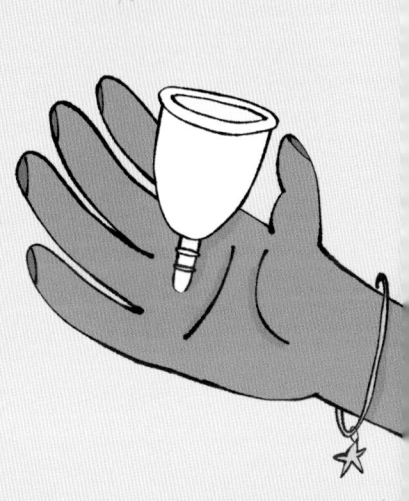

A WORD OF WARNING

Toxic Shock Syndrome (TSS) is a rare but serious infection that can happen when you use tampons or menstrual cups. If you suddenly feel extremely ill and your symptoms include a high temperature, shivers, feeling or being sick, diarrhoea, severe pain or a rash, contact a doctor right away.

If you've been using a tampon or a menstrual cup, take it out and tell the doctor you've been using one. You can reduce the risk of TSS by washing your hands before inserting tampons and menstrual cups. Don't use a tampon with more absorbency than you need, and ideally change it every 4-6 hours.

QUIZ: WHAT'S RIGHT FOR YOU?

Can't decide what product to use? This flow (see what we did there?) chart quiz might help to point you in the right direction!

IT'S NOT JUST YOU

If the thought of choosing between sanitary towels and tampons makes your head spin, don't worry – it can all seem a little daunting at first. But you don't have to pick one and stick with it. By trying out different products, you'll work out which one is right for you!

THE GREAT PERIOD PROTECTION FLOW DIAGRAM!

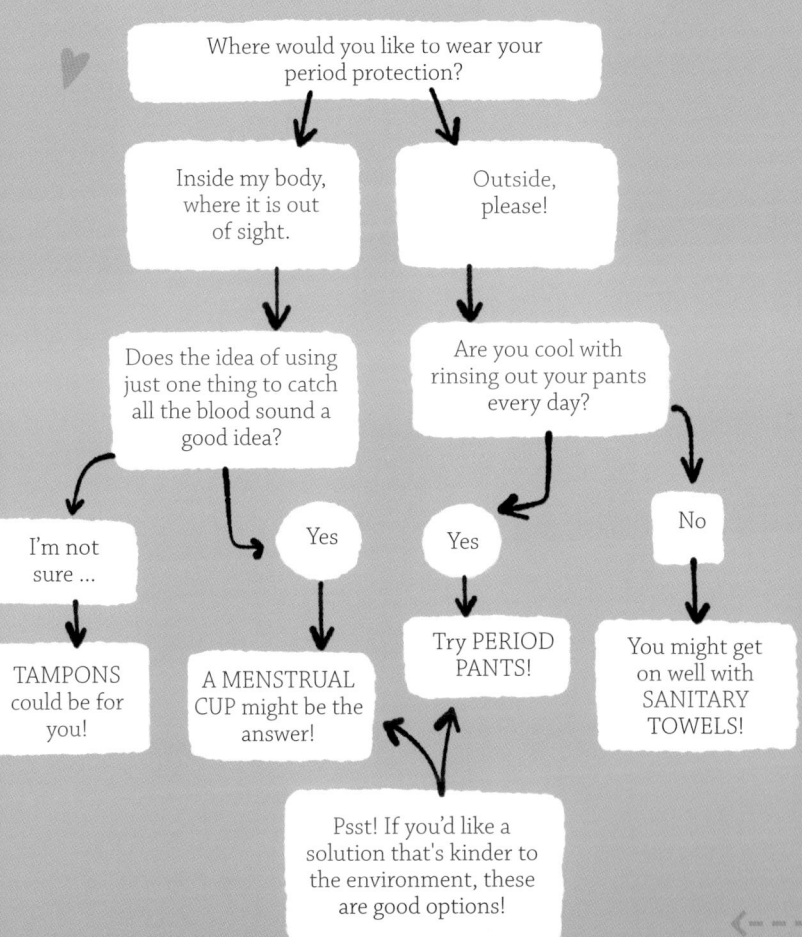

Where would you like to wear your period protection?

Inside my body, where it is out of sight.

Outside, please!

Does the idea of using just one thing to catch all the blood sound a good idea?

Are you cool with rinsing out your pants every day?

I'm not sure ...

Yes

Yes

No

TAMPONS could be for you!

A MENSTRUAL CUP might be the answer!

Try PERIOD PANTS!

You might get on well with SANITARY TOWELS!

Psst! If you'd like a solution that's kinder to the environment, these are good options!

PESKY PMS

You might have heard other girls and women mention PMS. And they probably didn't look super thrilled when they were talking about it.

Maybe they were even rolling their eyes. This is because PMS is often considered to be a bit of a nuisance. So what is it?

PREMENSTRUAL SYNDROME

PMS is short for Premenstrual Syndrome. It might sound like the name of an insurance company or a type of digger, but it's actually the name for the collection of symptoms that can appear before a period arrives. Medical people think PMS might happen when hormone levels suddenly change. Here are a few symptoms.

Mood swings

Anxiety

Tiredness

Anger

Headaches

Spots

Sore breasts

Bloating

But, KEEP CALM. Although you may experience one or two of these symptoms, there's absolutely no guarantee that you will get any. And you'd be very unlucky indeed to get all of them. Or you might get different symptoms every month, just to mix things up a little! And one good thing about PMS is that it can be a handy reminder that your period is just around the corner. An even better thing is that symptoms will start to improve once your period starts!

PAINFUL BLEEDING

About a tenth of girls and women suffer from endometriosis. This happens when tissue similar to the lining of the uterus grows in other parts of the body. The pain it causes can be confused with period pain as they often happen at the same time. Endometriosis can also cause heavy bleeding, bloating and tiredness. If you have very painful periods, do visit a doctor. They can help!

FACT OR FICTION?

If you're in a bad mood, it must be PMS.

FICTION!

It might be, but there's also a very good chance it isn't PMS. It's totally OK to be in a bad mood just because a brother or sister or a friend has annoyed you, and for it to be nothing to do with hormones!

FEELING GREAT DURING YOUR PERIOD

It's quite common to feel a low-down ache for the first couple of days of your period.

Menstrual pain – also known as period cramps – is caused when the uterus's muscles squeeze to push out period blood, which is why the pain comes and goes. So what's the best thing to do if it happens?

A HOT WATER BOTTLE

Hugging a hot water bottle really can help. The warmth from the hot water bottle helps to relax the uterus's muscles, reducing the pain.

EXERCISE!

Believe it or not, a great thing to do when period cramps hit is something active. This doesn't have to mean an extreme obstacle course or a triathlon – unless you want to, of course! Just something that gets you moving will do. Experts disagree over whether exercise actually reduces symptoms, but as physical activity has been proven to make you feel good, why not go for it anyway?!

FACT OR FICTION?

Eating chocolate helps to reduce period pain.

Quite possibly a FACT!

Many studies show that eating chocolate during your period can help to reduce period pain. But before you grab the nearest bar of super-deluxe extra-creamy milk chocolate, there's one teeny tiny drawback. It only works for dark chocolate. This contains magnesium, which helps to relax muscles. There's copper in there too, which may also ease symptoms.

(Psst! Bananas, oranges, avocados, wholegrains, beans, lentils, nuts, seeds, yoghurt, salmon, chicken and tofu may also help!)

WHAT ABOUT BOYS?

Girls aren't the only ones who go through puberty – boys do too! They don't get periods, but their bodies change in different ways.

Puberty for boys is also fuelled by hormones, but for them the main ingredient is testosterone.

BODY CHANGES

During puberty, boys grow in quite a different way. Testosterone makes the testicles grow and produce sperm. The penis gets larger, too. Like girls, boys get pubic hair, but this grows above the penis and on the scrotum – the pouch of skin that holds the testicles. Later, hair starts to grow under boys' arms and on their faces. They can decide whether to shave their facial hair or grow a cool beard instead.

DEEP DOWN ...

Meanwhile, a boy's larynx becomes bigger. This is where sound is created and it's located in the throat. Also known as the voice box, as the larynx increases in size, a boy's voice deepens.

If you want to find out more about what happens to boys in puberty, or help a male friend to get the right information, there's a 'Grow up Great' book for them, too!

FACT OR FICTION?

Boys' voices break.

Sort of FICTION and FACT!

Their voices don't actually break, of course. They still work afterwards. This is just what people say when a boy's larynx is growing bigger, which makes it hard to control the new sound of their voice. At this time, it might go up and down unexpectedly, before it eventually deepens into the voice they'll have as a man.

EMOTIONS ALL OVER

It's not just your body that changes during puberty. The way your brain works changes, too. But because your emotions develop BEFORE your ability to control your emotions better, this can leave you feeling a bit mixed-up.

MOOD SWINGS

Extreme emotions are very common during puberty, and they can change very quickly, too. One minute, you might feel on top of the world and the next you could be down in the dumps. There might be a perfectly good reason for your mood changes. Perhaps a parent is telling you off. Maybe you're already overloaded at school and you're given yet more homework. Perhaps a friend has said something mean about the way you look. But mood swings can also happen for absolutely no reason at all. If they do, go easy on yourself. You're not alone.

A TRICKY TIME

It's not just puberty that can make it difficult to be
an adolescent. As you get older, new experiences will
happen all the time. Some might be easy to deal with.
Others can be more difficult and kick off a range of
emotions. For example, peer pressure – when people
around you try to make you do things – can make you
feel anxious. Big tests and exams might make you feel
stressed. And what if you really like someone and don't
know whether they like you or not ...?

If you're feeling stressed or anxious for any reason,
try to find something that helps you to cope. It might
be a wild game of netball or blowing a trumpet REALLY
HARD. But you can also talk to someone about it,
whether it's a trusted adult or a school counsellor.
They'll be able to help.

FEELING OKAY OR NOT OKAY

During puberty, it's especially important to look after your mental health. While mood swings are absolutely normal, more extreme emotions could be a sign that there's a bigger problem. If this is the case, there's plenty of support available.

DEPRESSION

Depression is a mental health condition that can mean you feel very low for a long time, rather than something that comes and goes. Depression can change the way you think, feel and behave. It can affect different areas of your life too, from home and school, to your friendships.

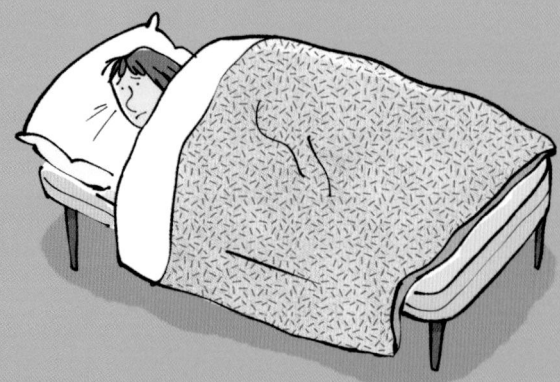

In young people, depression can be caused by problems such as bullying, a family break-up or changes, like moving house. But it can also sometimes be something you inherit. School counsellors have been trained to help those who are suffering from depression, anxiety or stress, and can help them to work out how to get better.

IMPORTANT!

If you are worried about your mental health, it's important to talk to a trusted adult. If you'd rather not talk to someone that you know, ask to speak to a school counsellor or go to page 95 for details of organisations that can help you.

DEALING WITH YOUR FAMILY

You might sometimes feel as if your family or the people you live with are more than a little irritating. If so, you are definitely not the first person to think this!

GRRRR!

Whether it's a parent invading your bedroom and telling you to get off the Internet right now and do some homework or asking you if you're really going out wearing THAT or a younger sibling borrowing your things without asking, all families can be annoying from time to time.

Even though they've obviously been through puberty themselves, parents don't always remember what it's like. They might also have forgotten that someone who is going through puberty might already be dealing with a whole bunch of stuff. And if that person is feeling glummer than someone who's just discovered that the biscuit tin is empty, then it's not a brilliant idea to annoy them further.

When this happens, try not to get too angry with them. Instead, breathe deeply before reacting. Then tell them how you're feeling. It really might help ... both them and you!

IT'S NOT JUST YOU

Part of growing up is discovering that you have your own opinions, thoughts and ideas. You might start to think that, actually, you don't need to do everything that a grown-up might say. Meanwhile, parents are used to the younger version of you and might carry on treating you as if you're still a child. It might take a while for everyone to adjust to the new dynamic, but keep talking until you do.

GROW YOUR CONFIDENCE

You probably know someone who seems out-of-this-world amazing.

They might have clear skin and hair like silk. They could be so full of confidence that they don't think twice about standing up in front of the entire school and giving the best speech ever about climate change. And when they play hockey, they're guaranteed to be the best at that, too. In short, they're perfect. Whereas you ... aren't. Or that's what you might be tempted to think.

FOCUS ON YOU

Sometimes, it might feel as if everyone is more fabulous than you. But that doesn't mean they actually are. Perhaps they wish they were taller or had curly hair or were a whizz at algebra. Rather than comparing yourself to everyone else, focus on what's awesome about YOU, right now.

Here are seven ways of improving your self-confidence. There's one to try every day of the week!

1. Remind yourself what you're FABULOUS at doing.
2. Do things that you love!
3. Try new things (you might discover that you love these, too!).
4. Pretend that you're confident (even if you're not).
5. Try to stand up for yourself.
6. You don't have to be superhuman. If you feel like having a lazy afternoon with a book, do it!
7. Find the nearest mirror, give yourself a big, hearty grin and remember that you're GREAT.

BUILD YOUR BODY IMAGE

When you're growing up, it's very easy to worry about the way you look. You might feel self-conscious about the changing shape of your body, your weight, your hair or anything, really.

And one thing that really doesn't help can be ... other people.

'PERFECT' CELEBRITIES

When there are endless images of perfect-looking people on social media, it's natural to compare yourself to them. But celebrities obviously don't get out of bed looking like that. It takes a lot of time, money, effort and fancy filters to turn them into such beautiful people. There's no way they could look so unbelievably awesome in time for school, five days a week. If you had a stylist, a hairdresser, a make-up artist and a fashionista living in your wardrobe, you'd always look red carpet-ready too.

'HELPFUL' RELATIVES AND FRIENDS

It's easy for other people to tell you not to be so silly because you look amazing. (Especially if it's a family member who always thinks you're fabulous, even if you have a spot the size of a small volcano on your nose.) Meanwhile, inspirational talks packed with confidence-building clichés that say everyone is beautiful might not always make you feel better. Other people mean well, but sometimes it's difficult to believe them. (Even when they're right.)

But there's one person who knows all about you. (That's YOU, by the way.) So ask them. Make a list of ten things you like about yourself. Look in a mirror and see what's great about your appearance! Self-confidence is all about what you think of yourself. It might be difficult, but try to avoid comparing yourself to other people and remind yourself what's good about YOU.

FRIENDSHIPS

Friends can be fabulous for many, many reasons. Here are just a few ...

- **They make you laugh.**
- **They don't judge.**
- **They're always ready to help.**
- **They know what you're going through, often because they're going through it themselves.**
- **They like you?**

OLD FRIENDS AND NEW FRIENDS

Puberty can be a challenging time for friendships. You're not the only one who's changing – your friends are too. So even though your best friend might be someone you met on your very first day of school, they may suddenly become hugely annoying. Perhaps they won't stop talking about boys. Or maybe they seem really childish. On the other hand, they may think that you're acting weirdly and they'd rather not start talking about which school subjects to pick right now, thank you.

There's no law that says you have to be best friends with the same person for your whole life. And when everyone develops at different rates, there are bound to be upsets. If friendships fizzle out, don't worry. They'll be replaced by new ones.

FACT OR FICTION?

When you move house or school, making new friends is really difficult.

FICTION!

Leaving all your friends behind might seem the worst thing in the world. But moving to a new place or going to a different school doesn't have to be as bad as it sounds. Even if you feel horribly shy, take a deep breath and try to talk to people. Join new groups and clubs. Play a team sport! You might find new friends sooner than you think.

FRIENDS OR ENEMIES?

Friendships don't always run smoothly. There may be times when a friend is mean to you or when you've accidentally upset them. Or perhaps you disagree over something BIG. What happens then?

CROSS WORDS

It would be pretty unbelievable if everyone agreed with each other all of the time. Politicians don't, and friends are no different. If you do argue with a friend, it can be a great way to get things out in the open. But it can be upsetting, too. Here are some things to remember the next time you argue with a friend.

1. Don't get mad.
If you stay calm, it'll be easier to deal with the argument in a reasonable way. But if you get angry, call your friend names and make an enormous fuss, it's going to be far harder to sort things out later.

2. Keep it between the two of you.
If it's an argument between you and your friend, there's no need to involve anyone else. If you do, the row will just become bigger and messier.

3. Take a break.
If things get out of hand, have a breather. Then talk about things logically when you've both calmed down.

4. Think carefully.
It takes two to argue. Could you be at fault? And is there anything you can do to help the situation?

After a row, it might be time to make friends again. You can talk, listen, apologise or do all three. But, sometimes, an argument can be a sign that you'd be better off apart. You might both find new friends that you get along with better!

BULLYING

Bullying is one of the most upsetting things that can ever happen to you, whether you're going through puberty or not.

People who bully do what they do because they're not in a good place. They might feel sad or insecure. Someone might be bullying them. Hurting other people is a way for them to feel powerful.

Bullying is hurting someone again and again. It can be physical – such as shoving, hitting or attacking someone. It can be verbal – such as name-calling or shouting at someone. It can be psychological – such as spreading rumours or saying hurtful things to someone to make them feel bad.

Bullying can happen in real life or online. And people who bully can act alone or as part of a group.

HOW TO DEAL WITH BULLYING

Don't be tempted to fight back against people who bully. This will just make things worse – you might get into trouble and you might be hurt. It might sound like a scary thing to do, but the best way of dealing with bullying is to tell a trusted adult what's going on and let them deal with it. Meanwhile, do your best to ignore the bully. Walk away from them. People who bully do what they do because they want you to react. If you act like you don't care, you'll ruin their fun.

FACT OR FICTION?

Bullying is just something you've got to put up with.
100% FICTION!
Bullying is totally unacceptable. In countries around the world, there are anti-bullying days, weeks and months to raise awareness of bullying and the harm it can cause. If it's happening to you, you do NOT have to put up with it. Tell someone you trust that it's happening, now.

THE HIGHS AND LOWS OF BEING ONLINE

You might be on social media ... you might not. It can be a great way of communicating with your friends, but it's important to remember that it's very different from talking in real life.

THE HIGHS

Social media apps allow you to send messages, pictures and videos to and fro. Because it doesn't take much effort, it's easy to tell others what you're thinking or doing. Meanwhile, these apps are also great platforms for sharing news, information or just things that make you laugh.

THE LOWS

But it's not all good. The problem with text messages is that it's sometimes not clear how something is being said. Messages that are meant to be funny might be taken the wrong way. Sometimes, people write messages that make them sound as if they're annoyed, when they really aren't. There's also a danger of seeing inappropriate content online; this can be very upsetting and should always be reported.

IT'S NOT JUST YOU

If you've received nasty messages via social media apps, or if others share photos of you without asking, don't keep it to yourself. Cyberbullying is a serious issue and even if it doesn't seem like bullying, it is. It's also illegal and can be tracked. Here's what you can do to stop it:

- Tell a trusted adult at once.
- Don't respond to messages.
- Block or unfollow the cyberbullies.
- Increase your privacy settings.
- Have a break from social media.

FUNNY NEW FEELINGS

As you grow older, you might start to have different feelings about people. You might notice someone's sparkling eyes, the way they smile or their great sense of humour. Just thinking about them can make you feel warm inside. You might want to hug or kiss them. When you feel this way, it's called a crush.

CRUSHES

If you develop a crush on someone you see all the time, you might suddenly feel very awkward around them. Even if you found it perfectly easy to talk to them before, you might now talk gibberish or totally forget how to speak whenever they appear. (It's no easier if your crush is a celebrity. Then all you can do is gaze at photos of them and wonder how much pocket money you'll need to save to fly to Hollywood.)

Crushes are totally normal and so are the feelings that go with them (but if you don't feel this way about anyone, that's perfectly OK too). Sometimes, the crush will go away or you might find an entirely new person to have a crush on instead. Sometimes, you'll decide to find out if your crush feels the same way, and would like to be your boyfriend or girlfriend.

IT'S NOT JUST YOU

Sometimes, the person you have the world's biggest crush on ... doesn't feel the same way about you. This can make you feel pretty bad. It's not nice being rejected, but it happens. If you're on the receiving end, just do your best to accept it and move on.

You never know. There could be someone REALLY fabulous just around the corner!

LOVE ETC

If you have a boyfriend or a girlfriend, there are lots of new things to think about. How often will you see them? Where will you hang out? What will you do together?!

DON'T SKIP THIS BIT!

A very important part of a relationship is making sure that you both agree with what you do together. Always check to make sure. For example, if you want to kiss the other person, ask them first. And never feel pressured into doing anything that you don't want to do. In a healthy relationship, both of you trust each other. You communicate well, are honest with each other and feel respected, safe and valued.

You know that you don't have to be together 24/7. And you know that it's OK to have other friends and spend time apart. If your relationship doesn't feel like this, then it might be time to rethink it.

FACT OR FICTION?

If you don't have a special someone, you're a failure.

FICTION, obviously.

Sometimes, it might feel like this, especially when it seems like all of your friends are dating someone. But it's really not true. Some people grow up faster than others. And boys usually start puberty later than girls. But being in a relationship simply doesn't make you a better person. It's YOU that makes you amazing – not the person you are or aren't dating.

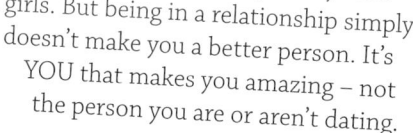

IT'S (NOT ACTUALLY THAT) COMPLICATED

Girls who have crushes on boys are known as 'heterosexual' or 'straight'. Girls who have crushes on girls are known as 'lesbian' or 'gay'. And girls who have crushes on both are known as 'bisexual'. These are all examples of sexual identity.

HOW ABOUT YOU?

You might already know who you like and what you are. But if you're not yet sure of your sexual identity – or don't think you'll ever know for sure – this is 100 per cent fine. These decisions are very personal and aren't always things you can decide just like that.

For some people, it takes a very long time to work out the answers. More than anything else, the important thing is to be happy and true to yourself.

TELLING PEOPLE

If you've decided to tell friends and family any decisions you've made about yourself, it can be nerve-wracking. So why not write down the things you want to say before you start? Try to think about the questions you might be asked, so you can be ready with answers.

However you identify yourself, remember that there are always people who can support and help you. You'll find some of them at the end of this book!

QUIZ

When did same-sex marriage become legal in the UK?

A: 1969   B: 1974   C: 2014

ANSWER C: 2014

It's not as long ago as you might think!
In most countries around the world,
same-sex marriage remains illegal.

FUEL YOUR BODY!

During puberty, it's super important to eat well. This means eating enough healthy food to fuel the huge amounts of developing and growing going on.

GROWING UP SO FAST!

Adults absolutely love saying this and you're probably completely fed up of hearing it, but it's true. However, did you know that although children grow quickly, they grow even faster during puberty? For girls, there's a growth spurt that happens a year or two before their periods start. When it happens, get ready to rocket upwards at a rate of 8 cm a year. Around this time, it's not unusual for girls to be taller than boys, who tend to have a growth spurt about two years later. Once your periods have started, you might grow a few more centimetres, but not as quickly.

If you find that you are hungrier, this is your body reminding you to eat more. This extra food helps you to grow faster. But it's important to eat healthy food from a variety of different food groups. These provide the nutrition you need to grow, while still giving you the energy to do all the usual things like going to school, riding a bike, shopping, being sporty and arguing with your siblings.

QUIZ

Can you guess which of these food groups isn't super healthy?

A: Wholegrain pasta and bread
B: Fruit and vegetables
C: Boiled sweets, candy floss and fizzy drinks
D: Milk, cheese, yoghurt or non-dairy alternatives
E: Fish, chicken, lean meat, eggs, beans and chickpeas

ANSWER: It's C, of course! These treats contain a lot of refined sugar, which gives a quick blast of energy, but doesn't contain anything nutritious. Too much sugar can lead to tooth decay, obesity, type 2 diabetes and heart disease.
(Psst. Simply swapping from sugary drinks to water cuts your sugar intake massively!)

FIT AND STRONG

Exercise is great way for everyone to be fit and healthy, and it's a really good thing to do while you're going through puberty.

Everyone under 18 should aim for at least an hour of exercise a day. And before you cover your ears and start saying LA-LA-LA, that doesn't mean an hour of gymnastics or running a 10K before breakfast. (Though if you feel like it, go for it!) It means a mixture of moderate and vigorous exercise. Here are some examples of both.

Moderate exercise is when you can still chat while you're doing it, but not sing.

- Walking the dog
- Riding a bike somewhere flat
- Scooting (but not on an electric scooter, because that would be ridiculous)
- Yoga.

Vigorous exercise is when you're properly out of breath.

- Dancing
- Football
- HIIT workouts.
- Running
- Swimming

WHY EXERCISE?

How long have you got?! Exercise is SO good
for you. It does all the obvious things, such as
making your heart stronger, building muscle and
increasing bone strength. But it does lots of surprising
things, too. Exercise gives your brain a workout, helping
you to think more clearly. It makes you feel happier
and reduces stress levels. It helps you to sleep better.
Bizarrely, it even gives you MORE energy!

IT'S NOT JUST YOU

If you don't think exercise is for you, think again. Not
everyone wants to dangle off a mountain or dive into
a rugby scrum. But there are LOTS of other options.
Perhaps Zumba is for you. Or ice-skating. Or tai chi!
Find something that YOU enjoy ... and have fun!

LEAVING PUBERTY BEHIND

Just as puberty doesn't start on an exact day,
it doesn't end on one either. You don't wake up one
day and say, 'Woohoo! I'm a grown-up!'. So how are
you meant to know that puberty's over?

KNOW THE SIGNS

If your breasts are fully developed, that's a
pretty good sign that the puberty finishing
line is in sight. This basically means that
you've been the same bra size for a while
and your bra fits well. Another telltale sign
is that you've stopped growing taller. When
your periods start, it's absolutely normal
for them to be all over the place. But when
periods become more regular – when they are
spaced fairly evenly – this can also show that
puberty is nearly done and dusted.

GROWING UP GREAT!

Puberty is a little like the chrysalis stage that a caterpillar goes through before it becomes a butterfly. While it's happening, lots of huge changes take place that slowly transform you into an adult. Some of the change you and others can see. But, just like the chrysalis, much is hidden. No one can see the development of your reproductive system and your brain. And no one can see the emotions that ping about inside you.

So if you're ever fed up with all the spots and periods and mood swings and grown-ups telling you what to do (AND HOMEWORK!) that you have to deal with during puberty, take a moment to give yourself a pat on the back. Then remind yourself that, just like a butterfly, you are …

growing up great!

GROWING UP GREAT FAQS

DO I HAVE TO USE TAMPONS?!
I CAN'T MAKE THEM WORK!

If you've tried to use tampons with no success, you're not alone. You don't have to be a magician to use them, but there is a knack. And if you've just started your periods, then you're already getting used to a completely new experience and it might not be a good time to learn a new skill, too. Instead, wait a few months and then have another go. Before you try, see if you can work out exactly where the tampon is meant to go – you could use a mirror to check where your vagina actually is – and then pick a time when you're more relaxed. If you wait until your period has started, then it might slide in a little easier too. And don't forget that if tampons aren't for you, there are lots of other options to choose from. (Visit pages 46-51 to find out more!)

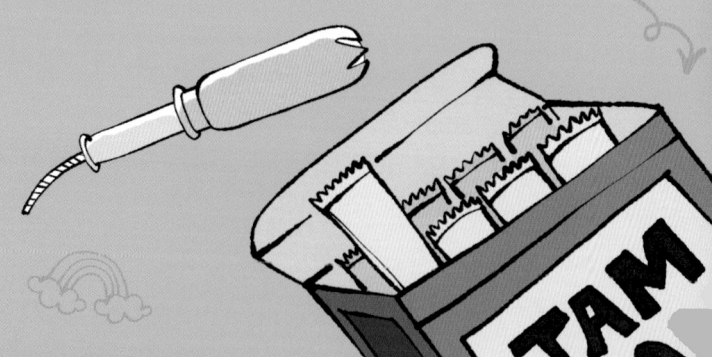

WHY AREN'T MY PERIODS REGULAR?

This is a question that doctors are asked all the time, and it has a very straightforward answer. Quite simply, it can take years for your reproductive system to operate like a well-oiled machine. But once your hormones have learnt how to work well together, your periods should happen more regularly. You might never know exactly when they're going to start, but if you keep a diary of when your periods begin, you should start to get a rough idea.

I'M NINE. IS IT NORMAL TO HAVE SMELLY ARMPITS ALREADY?

Yes! Body odour shows that puberty has begun, and can start when you're as young as seven or eight years old.

MORE GROWING UP GREAT FAQS

WHY DO MY LEGS ACHE SO MUCH AT NIGHT?

Aching or throbbing muscles in both legs is a condition that is common in children. Weirdly, although it's known as growing pains, medical people now think that it's nothing to do with your legs getting longer. But it's also nothing to worry about! If it's happening to you, massaging your legs or using a hot water bottle can help to ease the pain.

EVERY SINGLE GIRL IN THE WHOLE UNIVERSE HAS STARTED THEIR PERIODS, EXCEPT ME. WHAT'S WRONG WITH ME?!

It's SO annoying when this happens. It can feel as if everyone but you is in a secret club and there's no way of joining. But periods can start as late as 17, so it absolutely doesn't mean that there's anything wrong with you. Sometimes, late periods can be caused by stress, being underweight or if you do a huge amount of exercise. It's a good idea to talk to your doctor if your periods haven't started by the time you're 16.

THERE'S STICKY STUFF IN MY PANTS. IS THIS NORMAL?!

This is vaginal discharge. Your vagina is meant to be moist and sometimes the fluid leaks out. It's totally normal.

CAN I GO SWIMMING WHEN IT'S MY PERIOD?

Yes! Don't swim if you're using a sanitary towel as this could leak into the swimming pool. But period swimwear is ideal! You can also swim when you're using a tampon or a menstrual cup. Dive in and have fun!

EVEN MORE GROWING UP GREAT FAQS

IS IT NORMAL FOR MY BREASTS TO HURT?

Yes! Breasts can be tender when they're developing. They can also be sore around the beginning of a period. It happens because of the hormones zinging around your body.

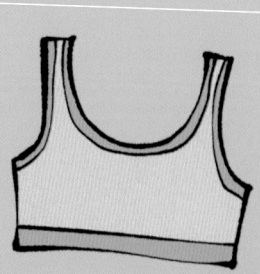 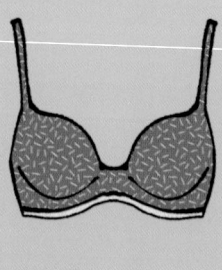

I'VE GOT SO MANY SPOTS THAT I LOOK LIKE A LEOPARD. WHAT CAN I DO?!

While they're going through puberty, most people suffer from acne – the skin condition that causes spots. But sometimes it can be quite bad. If you have lots of painful spots on your chest, back and face and these are making you feel sad, a doctor can help. They are able to prescribe medicines or creams or they can send you to see a dermatologist – an expert in skin conditions. You don't just have to put up with it.

HELP! ONE OF MY BREASTS IS BIGGER THAN THE OTHER! WHYYYY?

If one of your breasts is bigger than the other, DON'T PANIC. They're like feet. Well, not exactly like feet. But just as you might have one foot very slightly bigger than the other, it's the same with your breasts. Most women have breasts that are two different sizes. So if you have one breast bigger than the other, then you're definitely not the only one.

USEFUL WORDS AND iNFO

Acne: a skin condition that causes spots.

Adolescent: a young person, who is no longer a child but not yet an adult.

Antiperspirant: a product used to prevent sweating.

Anxiety: a feeling of worry or fear.

Bacteria: tiny organisms found on your body. Bacteria combines with sweat to produce body odour.

Birth parents: the woman who gave birth to you and the man who helped to conceive you.

Bisexual: when you are attracted to people of both sexes.

BO: short for body odour.

Counsellor: somone who has been specially trained to help people talk through their thoughts and feelings.

Crush: a strong feeling of attraction to someone.

Dating: when two people are attracted to each other and spend lots of time together.

Deodorant: a product used to hide body smells.

Depression: feeling of sadness and emptiness that lasts for a long time.

Gay: when you are attracted to people of the same sex.

Gene: a chemical code passed down from your birth parents that determines characteristics like your height and hair colour.

Heterosexual: when you are attracted to people of the opposite sex.

Hormones: chemical signals that control the way your body develops.

Ligaments: tissue that connects bones together.

Masturbation: when you touch your genitals for pleasure.

Menstruation: another word for period.

Mood swing: a sudden emotional change, such as going from calm to angry.

Menstrual cup: a squidgy silicone cup that can be used during a period.

Oestrogen: one of the main hormones that drives puberty in girls and women.

PMS: short for Premenstrual Syndrome, these are symptoms that you may experience before a period.

Pubic hair: Hair that grows around the genitals.

Social media: Websites and apps that let you communicate and share content with others.

Books

Grow Up Great: All You Need to Know About Puberty for Boys by Tim Collins (Frankin Watts, 2025)

Don't Panic, it's Puberty!: A Guide for Girls by Anna Claybourne (Franklin Watts, 2024)

Puberty in Numbers by Liz Flavell (Franklin Watts, 2020)

Websites

www.healthforteens.co.uk/growing-up/puberty/
If you'd like to find out more about puberty, this NHS website is packed with helpful advice.

www.becomingateen.co.uk
This website has lots of super-helpful information about puberty, periods and sanitary products.

www.childline.org.uk
If you're a young person in the UK and you're worried about something, you can contact Childline online and by calling 0800 1111.

Note to parents and teachers: every effort has been made by the Publishers to ensure websites are suitable for children, that they are of the highest educational value, and that they contain no inappropriate or offensive material. However, because of the nature of the Internet, it is impossible to guarantee that the contents of these sites will not be altered. We strongly advise that Internet access is supervised by a responsible adult.

INDEX

First published in Great Britain in 2025
by Franklin Watts
Copyright © Hodder and Stoughton
Limited, 2025
Editor: Julia Bird
Designer: Peter Scoulding
Consultant: Dr Kristina Routh
HB ISBN: 978 1 4451 9037 2
PB ISBN: 978 1 4451 9039 6
An imprint of Hachette Children's Group
Part of Hodder & Stoughton

Carmelite House
50 Victoria Embankment
London EC4Y 0DZ
An Hachette UK Company
www.hachette.co.uk
www.hachettechildrens.co.uk
Printed in China
The authorised representative in
the EEA is Hachette Ircland, 8 Castlecourt
Centre, Castleknock Road, Castleknock, Dublin
15, D15 YF6A, Ireland (email: info@hbgi.ie)